# Trapped in Education

From leadership to running out of the classroom, a teacher's true tale from burnout to recovery.

Sheetal Smith-Batish

Trapped in Education
Copyright © 2024 by Sheetal Smith-Batish

All rights reserved. No part of this publication may be reproduced, distributed, or transmitted in any form or by any means, including photocopying, recording, or other electronic or mechanical methods, without the prior written permission of the author, except in the case of brief quotations embodied in critical reviews and certain other non-commercial uses permitted by copyright law.

Tellwell Talent
www.tellwell.ca

ISBN
978-0-2288-4262-0 (Hardcover)
978-0-2288-4261-3 (Paperback)
978-0-2288-4263-7 (eBook)

# TABLE OF CONTENTS

Dedication ..................................................................... vii
Preface ............................................................................ ix
Chapter 1    Who Am I? ............................................... 1
Chapter 2    A Typical Teaching Day ........................... 6
Chapter 3    From City to Countryside ....................... 9
Chapter 4    Pregnant Teacher in the COVID-19 Pandemic ............. 13
Chapter 5    The Day Everything Went Wrong ................. 16
Chapter 6    A Mental Breakdown .............................. 19
Chapter 7    Microaggressions .................................... 24
Chapter 8    I don't want to teach anymore ................ 28
Chapter 9    Therapy ................................................... 32
Chapter 10   Oxfordshire Mind, Banbury, Women's Support Group ... 37
Chapter 11   Spiritual Healing .................................... 40
Chapter 12   Whispers of Destiny—Meeting a Medium ....... 43
Chapter 13   Hypnotherapy ......................................... 46
Chapter 14   Preparing for an Ofsted Inspection ........ 50
Chapter 15   Busting the Ofsted Myths! ..................... 54
Chapter 16   Being a SENDCo ................................... 57
Chapter 17   Indian Women in Education—It Is Time for Justice ...... 62
Chapter 18   International Women's Day! ................... 65
Chapter 19   The Dual Role—Being a Mum and a Teacher .......... 68
Chapter 20   Embracing the Future ............................ 72

For all teachers past, present and future,

'Do the best you can until you know better.
Then when you know better, do better.'

—Maya Angelou

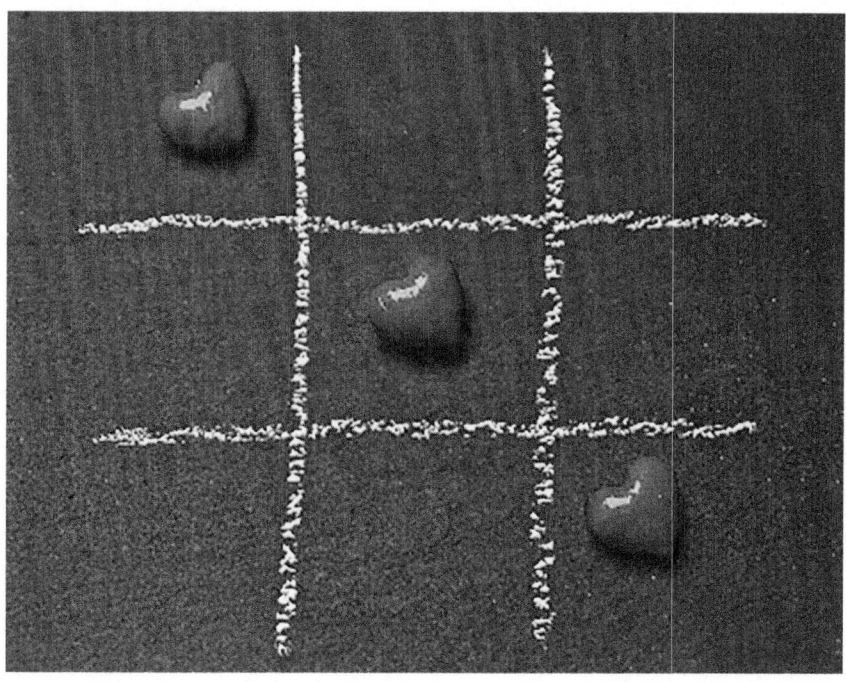

# DEDICATION

I would like to thank many people:
My dad, Sudesh Bhardwaj, for always believing in me and being there through my sickness and health: a true father.

My mum, Madhu Bhardwaj, for 'checking-in' on me daily, sending me health videos, and ensuring that I am well fed.

My boys, Reuben and Fabian, for giving me the inner strength required to recover mentally. I have built so much resilience and perseverance to build a better life for the three of us.

My sister, Priya Brar, for supporting me through my mental health recovery.

My cousin Komal Soni for taking the time to hear me on repeat during my darkest hours. My cousins Amit Sharma, Gita Kahlon, and her husband, Bally Kahlon, for giving me the strength to "keep calm and carry on!" My cousin Rohit Issar for supporting me in realigning my body and mind and bringing me back to the present.

My aunt, Pip Sharma, for listening to my troubles daily via video calls and giving me the courage to write this book. Thank you for proofreading, editing, and helping me publish my book.

My friends Deepak Sharma and Mandeep Chaggar for calling nearly every day to remind me how strong I am.

My wellness coach, Snehal Ghelani-Patel, for reaching out and reminding me to put myself first. Thank you for the chats, the meal plans, and the workout routines.

Fabian's key worker, Jo Bettles, for recognising that I was
not ok and for being there through my darkest days.

Pastor Jass Gil from Datchet Healing Spiritual Church for reminding
me of God's grace and powers and for bringing me back to reality.

My friend Lauren Hobbs, for listening when I needed a
good cry. I thank you for all the times you phoned.

My friends Kalpesh Patel, Rita Dugg, Shevell Stewart, and Damion
Rowsell, for always being there when I needed you, no matter what.

My counselling therapist for listening to my troubles
and giving me information about neuroscience. This
has taught me about my uncontrollable actions.

My neighbours Joanna Hunkin, Jen Styles, and Claire Nuzum for
being great friends and taking me out every time I needed some booze!

My friend, Jenni Wierchowicz for being there in
emergencies and when I need some pizza and wine.

My friend, Megan Ellison for understanding my mental
health condition and supporting me with recovery. Thank
you for all the prosecco and late-night chats.

I also thank 1st4Fitness, Bicester, and Louise Baily, for
reaching out during my time of need and tailoring a hybrid
programme flexible enough to weave through my hectic life.

The Deputy Headteacher I worked with for 10 years, Neil Handley
for teaching me everything I know about being successful in
Year 6 and the importance of integrity, honesty and support.

My new employer, a Catholic school in West London,
for giving me a lifeline, being there in my time of
need, and bringing my love for teaching back.

# PREFACE

'I am a Woman/Phenomenally/ Phenomenal Woman/that's me.'

—Maya Angelou

I qualified as a teacher in 2004 during the era of Numeracy and Literacy hour, LOGO programming and the dominance of PowerPoint presentations. Over my twenty successful years in education, I've had the privilege of working in ten different schools, ranging from city to countryside and from small village schools to large urban institutions with 1,500 children.

Each school has been a unique and rewarding experience for me. Unlike many, I find inspections exhilarating. They are opportunities to showcase my hard work. I'm passionate about promoting diversity, equality and mental health. I've been successful in driving school improvement and curriculum design and achieving the best pupil outcomes through Carol Dweck's growth mindset approach.

Unfortunately, the COVID-19 pandemic turned my world upside down. During this time, I isolated for two years due to pregnancy. When I returned to work, I suffered from chronic stress, post-traumatic stress disorder, dissociation, amnesia, and depression. My short-term memory suffered, leading to a referral to a neurologist who diagnosed me with chronic burnout, saying I had "broken my brain." Though it was a horrendous experience, I learned a lot about mental health, and now I want to share my story and raise awareness.

I've always broken the mould! As a young Asian female, I've reached many senior positions. I moved out of my family home before marriage. I married outside of my religion, race, and caste. I have mixed-race children and currently live in Oxfordshire, where my brown skin stands out and makes certain people uncomfortable.

This book aims to share my career journey, including the times when things went sour. I want people to hear my voice and understand the issues that affect many sectors, particularly mental health and microaggressions. There's a significant lack of understanding, compassion, and empathy in many areas of the system. People can be so self-absorbed that they forget about those around them.

It's no surprise that we're in the midst of a recruitment crisis with the lack of support in the sector causing many teachers to suffer from burnout and leave the profession they love.

No names of schools or individuals are provided in this book. Despite the challenges, I've thoroughly enjoyed working at each school. Due to working conditions and the staff dynamics, the chaos in my mind led to chronic stress and a mental health episode.

I hope this book helps educators and leaders to recognise the importance of wellbeing and taking relevant remedial action.

If you're going through a difficult time or experiencing a mental health episode, I hope you find the strength to seek recovery. Keep an open mind; there is so much out there to help.

## CHAPTER ONE

# Who Am I?

"There is no greater agony than bearing an untold story inside you."

—Maya Angelou

How Many Titles?

Year 6 Class teacher, Standard Assessment Tests External Marker, Newly Qualified Teacher Mentor, Senior Leader, Computing Leader, English Leader, Personal Social Health Emotional Lead, Relationships and Sex Lead, Special Educational Needs Disability Co-ordinator, Oxfordshire County Council Tutor, Key Stage Two Leader, Deputy Safeguarding Lead, Assistant Headteacher, Acting Headteacher, Shadow Ofsted Participant, Published Author, Trainee Counsellor, but most importantly … a MUM to my two boys.

My History

My name is Sheetal. I'm a mum of two little boys (Reuben, age ten, and Fabian, age three). To a class of Year 6 pupils, I'm Mrs Smith. I grew up in Southall, Middlesex, or like some used to say, 'I'm from Greenford, Ealing borough.' I'm fortunate to have parents who bring a rich cultural heritage from India and a large extended family full of aunts, uncles and a 'million' cousins. My family love to celebrate every occasion and 'party hard!' We're all 'foodies' and we love to dine out, sing and dance.

I'm the eldest of three siblings. My younger brother is the prankster, always ready with a joke or a mischievous grin, while my little sister has big, curious eyes and loves to sing and dance. Back in the day, we were inseparable, bound by a shared sense of adventure and a deep, unspoken bond.

Saturday nights were a sacred ritual in our household. As soon as the sun dipped below the horizon, my dad would return home with a bucket of KFC; the spicy aroma usually filled the house, tantalizing everyone's senses. We'd all gather in the living room, settling onto the plush, well-worn sofa, plates in hand, ready for a weekly dose of WWE. We were all avid fans of Bret 'The Hitman' Heart and the Bushwhackers!

I went to Lady Margaret Primary School and Greenford High School. My most vivid memory is visiting Shropshire in Year 6. I remember sitting by the fire and, at times on the windowsill in my bedroom, drawing in my art book. Back then I had a passion for art. Mr Eden, my art teacher, truly ignited my creative spark. He was a kind, soft-spoken man with an eye for talent. He invested a lot of time in providing me with guidance and feedback, pushing me to experiment with different techniques. His encouragement was a beacon of hope, and my biggest achievement was gaining an A at GCSE. Under his mentorship, my skills truly flourished. I spent countless hours perfecting my craft and often losing myself in the colours and textures of my work. The art room was my sanctuary, a place where I could express myself freely and explore the depths of my imagination. I wanted to be a secondary school art teacher but at the time, studying for an art degree wasn't accepted in Indian culture. It was all about studying medicine, law, engineering or dentistry.

My love for teaching began when I was seven years old. I would teach my younger siblings the water cycle, and I taught it with so much passion.

They hated studying but I loved it! I did the same lesson every time we played 'teachers!' I'd write all over my wooden cupboards and make my younger brother and sister draw and label the hydrological cycle. You can imagine how great I felt when I taught it for real!

I've now been teaching for twenty successful years, but my career turned sour post-pandemic. My journey as an educator began with a blend of excitement and nerves. As a newly qualified teacher, I started my career at a junior school in Southall. This vibrant and multicultural school, with its four hundred children speaking a myriad of languages, provided the perfect experience and gave me the opportunity to really make my mark. As a Year 6 class teacher and computing leader, I quickly adapted to the dynamic environment, where many pupils had English as an additional language.

My headteacher at the time was a nurturing presence. She was often likened to a mother by the staff. She maintained a positive and happy atmosphere in the school and it was a place where teachers felt valued and they rarely left. She was particularly tech-savvy and saw great potential in me. She beamed with pride when I earned the prestigious Information Communication Technology (ICT) Mark, a testament to our dedication and skill in integrating technology into the classroom.

The early days were filled with challenges, like turning on all the PCs and hoping to get the LOGO programming language to work for the afternoon lessons. Despite these hurdles, I thrived in the supportive environment, learning to navigate and innovate with the resources at hand.

After a decade in Southall, I moved on to an academy in Hayes. The transition was stark. The new school had a different atmosphere with a more insular staff and a predominantly White British pupil population. The teaching methods were rigid and the environment felt less inclusive. Despite these challenges, I took on the role of English Lead with determination. I pursued and achieved the National Professional Qualification for Middle Leadership, significantly improving writing standards across the school. It was here where my spark for writing ignited.

Seeking a more harmonious setting, my next move was to a Catholic school in Northolt. It was where I wanted my son Reuben to attend. From the moment I walked in, I was struck by the calm and peaceful atmosphere, epitomized by the statue of Mary at the entrance. The school offered a perfect blend of academic rigor and spiritual reflection, with regular times for prayers and contemplation. I found solace and inspiration in this environment, relishing the opportunity to blend my professional skills with personal growth.

However, life had other plans. My husband desired a change of pace, wishing to raise our children in the countryside for a better quality of life. We relocated to Upper Heyford in Oxfordshire, a place rich in history and natural beauty. Our new home was built on a former American RAF air base. It provided a fascinating glimpse of the past. I found joy in overlooking the fields, especially during the tranquil winter months when we were snowed in.

In September 2017, I began working at a small village school in Oxfordshire as a class teacher for Years 5/6. The school, with its picturesque classroom overlooking the fields, became my sanctuary. I loved the fresh air that filled the room and felt a deep connection with the village community. The children, so different from the streetwise kids in London, brought a refreshing innocence to my teaching experience.

Despite the initial cultural shocks, such as the children not knowing who Stormzy, Martin Luther King, or Rosa Parks were, I quickly found my stride. I embraced the opportunity to introduce these important figures and concepts to my students. Over time, I became an integral part of the school community, leading values assemblies and taking charge of the school curriculum.

In this small village school, I found my "forever school." The sense of fulfilment derived from my work was unparalleled. My journey from a bustling junior school in Southall to this serene countryside school in Oxfordshire was marked by growth, adaptability, and unwavering dedication. I had come full circle, bringing with me the rich experiences and lessons learned along the way, ready to continue making a positive impact in the lives of my students.

There was so much I loved about teaching in the village. I adored my classroom with its expansive library of books and the cozy library itself. Leading English was a joy; fostering a reading culture and ensuring each child made good progress were my top priorities. The end-of-year gatherings in the village hall and the walks to the village church were my highlights.

In 2020, the pandemic hit and I went into isolation for two years. I was desperate to return to school because I loved being there. I missed the routine and being in my classroom with my pupils. During my time, I had accomplished so much. I had prepared each subject for an Ofsted Deep Dive and worked tirelessly to push the school toward an 'Outstanding' rating. My involvement in school improvement and raising standards across all subjects was significant. However, the pandemic altered my experience profoundly. I was out of public places for two years, unable to visit the school, and devoid of adult interactions. Life became very lonely.

This is my life…

# CHAPTER TWO

# A Typical Teaching Day

"We may encounter many defeats but we must not be defeated."

—Maya Angelou

A Day in Secondary Teaching: The Journey of Inspiring Minds

6:00 AM —The calm before the storm. The alarm buzzes, pulling me from my warm bed. I stretch and take a moment to mentally prepare for the day ahead. Teaching is not just a job; it's a calling that demands energy, creativity, and a positive mindset. After a quick shower and a hearty breakfast, I think about my lesson planning, get the kids ready, and we are go … go … go. Today's agenda: engaging my students in a discussion of Shakespeare's *Macbeth*, a science experiment on chemical reactions, and a math quiz on the four operations (addition, subtraction, multiplication, and division).

7:30 AM—The morning rush. I arrive at school, coffee in hand, and head straight to my classroom. The school is already buzzing with activity: students chatting in the hallways, teachers preparing their rooms, and the caretaker ensuring everything is in place. I unlock my classroom, arrange the desks, and write the day's objectives on the whiteboard. There's a certain magic in these early morning moments, a sense of potential and new beginnings.

8:45 AM—Setting the tone. The bell rings, and students file outside my room. We start with the register and Newsround. I check in with each student; a simple "How are you today?" can make a huge difference. Today, I notice T__ seems a bit down. I make a mental note to talk to him later.

9:00 AM—English class. Diving into Shakespeare. The first class of the day is English. Today, we're reading Act II of *Macbeth*. I split the class into groups and assign roles for a read-aloud session. The students enthusiastically embrace their parts, and I'm reminded of the power of literature to transport us to different worlds. We discuss themes of ambition and fate; the kids are truly engaged. Somehow, their answers always surprise me!

10:30 AM—Science class. The wonders of chemistry. Today's experiment involves mixing baking soda and vinegar to demonstrate a chemical reaction. The students are excited. They love hands-on activities. I walk around the room, guiding them and answering questions. Their faces light up as the mixture fizzes and bubbles over. We discuss the science behind the reaction, and I see their curiosity ignite. We use this method to make volcanoes at another date.

12:30 AM—Lunchtime. Lunchtime is a welcome break. I join my colleagues in the staff room, where we exchange stories and strategies. After a quick lunch, I use the remaining time to mark a few papers and prepare for the afternoon classes.

1:30 PM—Maths class. Tackling the four operations. After lunch, it's time for maths. Today's focus is on solving the four operations, in particular long division. I start with a brief review before handing out the quiz. As the students work, I walk around to offer encouragement and assistance. I see some struggling, but I remind them that making mistakes is part of the learning process. By the end of the class, most have grasped the concept, and their sense of accomplishment is palpable.

3:00 PM—Planning and Reflection. The final bell rings, signalling the end of the school day. I spend the next hour planning for tomorrow, reflecting on what worked well today and what didn't. Continuous improvement is key to effective teaching. I tweak my lesson plans, incorporate new ideas, and think of ways to engage my students even more.

4:00 PM—Heading home. As I pack up and head home, I feel a sense of fulfilment. Teaching is challenging, but it's also incredibly rewarding. Knowing that I've made a difference in my students' lives, even in small ways, keeps me motivated. I look forward to another day of learning, growing, and inspiring young minds.

Evening—Recharging for tomorrow. The evening is for family, relaxation, and a bit of self-care. I might read a book, watch a show, or simply unwind. As I drift off to sleep, I think about my students and the adventures that await us tomorrow. Each day in teaching is unique, filled with challenges and triumphs, and I wouldn't trade it for anything.

## CHAPTER THREE

# From City to Countryside

'You may shoot me with your words, you may cut me with your eyes, you may kill me with your hatefulness, but still, like air, I'll rise!' –

—Maya Angelou

The hum of the city was a constant companion for me. Born and raised in the lively neighbourhoods of West London, I thrived amidst the multicultural society and how I loved the pace of urban life. My classroom at a bustling London primary school was filled with students from diverse backgrounds, each bringing their unique stories and perspectives. I loved teaching in London. The children were 'street-wise,' 'tech-savvy' and I loved the fact that they knew a bit of hip-hop! I loved the dynamic energy, the challenge of teaching and the sense of purpose that came with shaping young minds. Yet a desire for change after having a child, a yearning for tranquillity and the attraction of a simpler family life had driven me to make a momentous decision—to move to the English countryside.

The picturesque village of Upper Heyford, with its rolling green hills, charming cottages, and a close-knit community, seemed like a perfect escape from the stress and chaos of city life. I imagined myself breathing in the fresh, unpolluted air, taking leisurely walks with my son in the countryside, and finding a new rhythm that harmonised work and personal wellbeing. Well, that was the plan.

However, reality proved to be far more complex than my idyllic vision.

The first few weeks were filled with a mix of excitement and apprehension. Heyford's serene beauty was undeniable, and the warm welcome from the locals was heartening. It was strange to walk down the street and see the residents smile and wave. In London, you'd look down to avoid an argument! But as the initial novelty wore off, I began to feel the stark contrasts more acutely. The silence that once seemed peaceful now felt oppressive. The slower pace I had longed for started to feel like stagnation. The once charming quirks of village life turned into daily frustrations.

In my London school, days were filled with lively discussions, diverse viewpoints, and the constant buzz of activity. Here, the rural setting came with its own set of challenges, limited resources, a conservative community resistant to new teaching methods, and a cultural gap that seemed to widen with each passing day. The initial excitement gave way to a sense of isolation.

The isolation wasn't just professional; it was deeply personal. My colleagues were polite but distant, their bonds forged over years of shared experiences. The casual invitations to local events felt more like formalities than genuine attempts at friendship. I missed the impromptu coffee chats with my friends, the vibrant street markets, and the diversity that had enriched my life in London. The loneliness began to creep in a silent but ever-present shadow, especially after the pandemic.

The pressure of adapting to a new environment while maintaining my teaching standards began to take a toll. I found myself working longer hours, trying to innovate within the constraints I faced, and striving to meet my own high expectations. Sleep became elusive, and my once-passionate approach to teaching started to feel like a burden. I missed the professional development opportunities, the stimulating conversations with fellow educators, and the sense of community I had left behind.

One particularly cold, grey morning, the weight of it all became too much. I found myself standing in front of my class, my vision blurring with tears as I couldn't hold back. The concerned faces of my students were a stark contrast to the vibrant, eager expressions I had cherished in London. The room seemed to close in on me; the walls of my once-dreamt-of sanctuary now felt like a prison.

I excused myself abruptly, leaving my bewildered students behind, and retreated to the staff room. The dam of emotions broke and I sobbed uncontrollably. It wasn't just the loneliness or the professional frustrations; it was the overwhelming sense of feeling that I had made a mistake. The dream of a peaceful life in the countryside had turned into a nightmare of isolation and despair.

My breakdown did go unnoticed. I managed to disguise my fears from the school community. Day by day, the workload and pressure I had put on myself took its toll. I began hallucinating and hearing noises. I wasn't sure what to do and ended up applying for and accepting a new job. I didn't want to leave, but after two years of nothingness, my calm brain became chaotic. I couldn't understand what was going on because I didn't know. The local GP diagnosed me with severe anxiety and depression, conditions exacerbated by my drastic life change. I was told that I was in the middle of a breakdown and diagnosed with post-traumatic stress disorder, dissociation, and amnesia.

Recovery was a slow and painful process. I sought therapy from MIND charity and a women's support group in Banbury. I made regular visits back to London to reconnect with friends and family. The realisation that it was okay to feel overwhelmed, to seek help, and to admit that things weren't working out as planned was a crucial turning point.

In time, I made the difficult decision to leave Heyford Park and return to London. The move wasn't a failure but a necessary step for my mental health and wellbeing. My experience in the countryside taught me valuable lessons about resilience, the importance of community and the need to align my environment with my personal and professional needs.

My story is a poignant reminder that change, no matter how well-intentioned, can bring unexpected challenges. It highlights the importance of mental health, the complexities of adapting to new environments and the courage it takes to recognise when a dream is not aligning with reality. Most importantly, it underscores the strength required to make the right choices for oneself, even when they are difficult and heart-wrenching.

## CHAPTER FOUR

# Pregnant Teacher in the COVID-19 Pandemic

> 'Life is not measured by the number of breaths we take, but by the moments that take our breath away,'
>
> — Maya Angelou

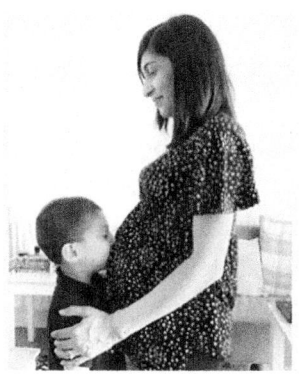

Being pregnant is inherently stressful, presenting a myriad of challenges from constant anxiety to relentless morning sickness, perpetual tiredness, and swollen feet. These symptoms, along with others, often catch women off guard until experienced firsthand. Now imagine navigating these hurdles as a teacher amidst a global pandemic. This piece stems from a restless night after tending to a nighttime feeding, prompting me to express gratitude to the supportive individuals around me while shedding light on the anxiety and strain pregnant women endure during antenatal appointments, where partners are not permitted to attend.

Discovering my pregnancy on my birthday in January brought me a great deal of joy. Though discussions about expanding our family had surfaced before, as a Year 6 teacher, timing never seemed right. Leaving my students amidst SATS preparations often left me feeling guilty. Yet upon learning of our impending addition, sheer elation washed over us. One of the first people I confided in was my headteacher; his support was pivotal, and I needed to explain my frequent classroom absences.

Soon after, severe morning sickness consumed my days, prompting numerous visits to the hospital for relief. Despite the toll it took, I persevered at work, maintaining a facade of normalcy while battling hormonal fluctuations and exhaustion. Then the pandemic struck, exacerbating anxiety levels. Concerns about the virus's impact on my unborn child loomed large, especially given the nature of my profession, which is a breeding ground for germs.

As the situation evolved, pregnant women were categorized as vulnerable, prompting my headteacher to close my class for my safety. Communicating this abrupt change to my students felt unnerving; for the first time, I lacked answers to their myriad questions about the uncertain future. Subsequently, the nationwide lockdown was announced, thrusting us into uncharted territory.

Amidst the chaos, my first scan offered a glimpse of joy, but restrictions meant my son wasn't able to with me at the appointment. Nevertheless, the sonographer's gesture of including his name on the scan picture eased the disappointment. Yet pregnancy-related symptoms persisted, intensifying with time. Balancing remote teaching, parenting, and homeschooling my six-year-old proved taxing, often triggering stress headaches.

As restrictions eased, my role transitioned to supporting my son's education while grappling with worsening pregnancy symptoms. Gestational thrombocytopenia added to my concerns, necessitating frequent hospital visits. Each appointment felt increasingly solitary, devoid of the familial support I craved.

Approaching the end of summer, I opted to begin my maternity leave early, grappling with physical discomfort and ongoing sickness. Despite the deviations from my envisioned pregnancy journey, the arrival of my son, Fabian, brought immeasurable joy. I cherish the opportunity to be a full-time mother, relishing in the simple pleasures of motherhood.

My gratitude extends to my partner, son, and the exceptional midwives who eased my labour experience. Yet the utmost appreciation is reserved for my headteacher, whose unwavering support and compassion guided me through pregnancy and beyond. His acts of kindness, from providing lemon water to checking in on my wellbeing, reaffirmed his exceptional leadership and genuine care.

# CHAPTER FIVE

# The Day Everything Went Wrong

"Nothing will work unless you do."

—Maya Angelou

I woke up feeling an unusual sense of foreboding. The sky outside was grey and heavy with the promise of rain and my alarm clock had failed me for the first time in years. As I hurriedly dressed and gulped down a cup of lukewarm coffee, I couldn't shake the feeling that today was going to be a challenge. I just didn't know how much of one yet.

Arriving at the school with minutes to spare, I rushed to my classroom, my thoughts racing ahead to the lessons I had meticulously planned. I had spent hours perfecting my presentation on the American Revolution, complete with interactive activities that I hoped would captivate my Year 8 history class. As I fumbled with my keys, the first raindrops began to splatter on the windows, creating a low, rhythmic tapping that seemed to mock my growing anxiety.

I entered the classroom to find chaos. The projector was missing. With a sinking heart, I remembered that it had been borrowed by the science department the previous day. A quick check confirmed my fears: the projector was still in the science lab. With no time to retrieve it, I had to improvise.

"Okay, class," I began, trying to keep my voice steady, "we're going to have a slightly different lesson today."

Groans and murmurs of discontent filled the room. It was clear that my students were not pleased. As I struggled to adapt my lesson plan to a chalkboard-only format, the class grew increasingly restless. The interactive activities I had planned were impossible without the technology I'd been counting on. Instead, I found myself scrawling bullet points on the board, watching my students' eyes glaze over.

Just when I thought things couldn't get worse, the fire alarm went off. The piercing screech sent everyone into a frenzy. I hastily led my class outside, where they joined the rest of the school on the muddy football field. The rain, which had started as a drizzle, was now pouring down in earnest. Students huddled together, shivering and complaining, while I struggled to maintain order.

After what felt like an eternity, they were finally allowed back inside. Drenched and disheartened, I resumed her lesson, only to be interrupted by the school intercom.

"Mrs Smith, please report to the principal's office immediately."

Leaving my class in the hands of the teaching assistant, I trudged to the principal's office, each step heavy with dread. As I entered, Principal Jackson looked up with a serious expression.

"Mrs Smith, we've had some complaints about your lesson today."

It turned out that some parents had called in, upset that their children weren't getting the full, interactive experience that had been promised at the beginning of the term. I tried to explain the situation, but Principal Jackson wasn't in the mood for excuses. I left the office feeling chastised and demoralised.

Returning to my classroom, I found that the teaching assistant had somehow managed to quell the chaos, but only barely. The students were still unsettled, their energy buzzing just below the surface. I attempted to salvage what was left of the period, but it was clear that my authority had been undermined.

As the final bell rang, releasing the students into the wilds of the schoolyard, I slumped into my chair. My clothes were still damp, my lesson a disaster, and my spirit thoroughly crushed. I stared at the stack of ungraded papers on my desk, feeling the weight of the day pressing down on me.

Suddenly, there was a knock at the door. I looked up to see Sarah, one of his quieter students, standing hesitantly in the doorway.

"Mrs Smith, I just wanted to say that I really liked the way you explained the causes of the American Revolution today. It made a lot of sense."

For a moment, the gloom lifted. It wasn't much, but it was enough to remind me why I loved teaching in the first place. Even on the worst days, the smallest victories could make all the difference.

With a faint smile, I thanked Sarah and watched her leave. Tomorrow was another day, and despite everything, I knew I'd be back, ready to try again.

# CHAPTER SIX

## A Mental Breakdown

'No matter what happens, how bad it seems today, life does go on and it will be better tomorrow.'

— Maya Angelou

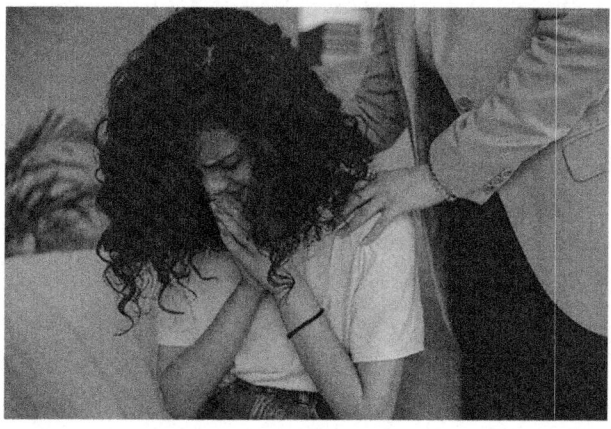

I love writing and have spent over a decade as an English curriculum leader. Among all the roles I've had, teaching children to write has been my forte. However, there came a time in my career when I couldn't read, write, or teach. Have you ever experienced a mental breakdown that left your class calling out your name, asking you to come back?

It all began in 2020, the year of the pandemic. In March, I was in my classroom, a place I adored. My school was in a beautiful village and my classroom overlooked a serene field. I loved the fresh morning air, the birds singing and occasionally walking to the small village church where we would gather to pray, sing or put on a show.

But March 2020 was different. I was sent home at the pandemic's onset because I was pregnant and very little was known about the virus, COVID-19. I didn't realise then that I would be in isolation for the next two years. It was like living in Groundhog Day: cleaning the house from top to bottom, walking around the block, soaking in the bath, and doing all the baby preparations. Soon my little boy, Fabian Asher Smith, was born at John Radcliffe Hospital on September 17, 2020. He was a lockdown baby who brought us immense joy but those times were hard with no visitors, no mum and baby groups, and no support. It was just me, a tired mum with a crying baby all day and night. Fabian spent more time in the hospital than at home due to lung infections, asthma and food intolerances.

Finally, the day came for me to return to work and I couldn't wait for some adult interaction after two years. But things took an unexpected turn. During the summer holidays, I was asked to return as a full-time Year 6 class teacher and an acting headteacher, lead an Ofsted inspection, manage staff conflicts and handle sleepless nights with a sick baby. I worked every night until 2:00 a.m, obsessed with achieving an 'Outstanding' rating for the school. Unfortunately, I didn't realise the toll it would take on me. I began hallucinating and became paranoid. One day I ran around the school hall telling everyone, "I am leaving!" I didn't realise I was leaving the school building for good. I felt disrespected and mentally exhausted, unable to let go of the disrespect I received for working so hard. I was fed up with pulling everyone up and not having time to be a mum. I was exhausted and had put too much on myself.

During the pandemic, the government had published guidance on improving reading and keeping children on track with expected progress. I contacted the school to ensure they implemented the changes, but school life was hard. People were scared for their lives and I had invested so much time in phonics that my brain became fixated on it. I spent hours each day producing documents on reading and my brain became stuck. It's a shame no one saw the damage inside my head. I didn't want to do all that work and then leave but I didn't realise what I was doing until it was done. Then it was too late. I remember leaving the school, feeling a puff of air hit my face, hearing a loud explosion in my head and seeing flashing lights. I couldn't register adults and pupils saying goodbye. I wasn't there anymore, just the screams in my head.

I decided to apply for another job because I wasn't coping. The problem was I went for an interview and then returned to work with no memory of the process. For the next year, my brain began to shut down. Despite my cries of "I am not okay," I was asked to write my resignation. I had applied for a job, asked for a reference, and attended an interview, but I didn't want to go. I didn't know I was leaving the school I loved forever. I just needed a break. After two years, I couldn't recognise sarcasm or rude comments while in a bad place. I took everything personally because I was mentally exhausted. I remember sitting at a child's desk in my room, hearing screaming in my head and running out of the door with all my belongings, never to return. I never wanted to leave the school, but I had been away for a long time and couldn't forgive the behaviour I faced in the absence of my headteacher. My mind and body disconnected and I was diagnosed with dissociation. I suffered from time distortion and couldn't recognise the consequences of my actions until they were done. There was a bang in my head every time I left the classroom, walked through the school doors, and when I got home. Leading the school had been so traumatic that my mind wiped any memory of the place I loved.

I joined a new school as if I had always been there. I remember sitting at my new desk so exhausted that I couldn't do anything. My memory was wiped. I couldn't remember the beginning of the term. All I could hear were screams. In May 2022, I came to work with my head pounding, unable to understand having SATS week in a different school. I was diagnosed with PTSD, amnesia, and dissociation. For the first time in twenty years, I was signed off. The brain fog left me feeling confused and forgetful. Conversations would fade from my memory instantly. Stress, depression and lack of sleep contributed to brain fog. I spent days, weeks, and months lying on the grass in my back garden, praying to live another day for my children.

Nights were hell. I longed for sleep but only heard the screams in my head. I was traumatised. Returning to work was hard and I couldn't keep the staff happy. I was disliked for having a temporary title, and it became very personal. Day by day, the days became unbearable and I hesitated to go in. Intimidating staff members made my mental health worse. Despite improving school standards and pupil results, my temporary title, brown skin, and drive were problems. My mental health was affected like never before due to the unexpected behaviour under pressure: being ignored, left out, lied about, criticised, and facing rumours. Everything around me became a blur. The worst part was receiving complaints while sitting in the hospital with my baby. I didn't want to work there anymore. I became fragile and lost. I just wanted to leave. It was the worst experience of my career. At the time, my brain felt under attack. I became paranoid and lost mentally.

For two years I jumped from post to post. I became a part-time SENDCo, worked for the council tutoring pupils with SEND in their homes, and became a supply teacher in a secondary school. Eventually I landed a job as an Assistant Headteacher in a secondary, independent SEMH school. I loved the calmness that followed: no drama, no more late nights, no more proving myself. I was trusted and given the break I needed. But mentally, I was still scarred.

Three years later, the trauma lingered. I could still hear the screams and the headaches wouldn't stop. Years of therapy helped, but my mind remained stuck. Floppy Phonics, Reading Deep Dive, Floppy Phonics, Reading Deep Dive. My brain was fixated on paperwork, unable to shift. I suffered from time distortion. My mind was stuck wanting to change a resignation email that I was told to write whilst unfit. My mind became obsessed with wanting to change the past. I left my poor class looking out of the window, shouting my name. Years later, I saw them in secondary school, all grown up. The hugs, tears and emotions overwhelmed me. "Why did you leave us? What happened?" I wasn't well. I wasn't well. I wasn't well. Why didn't anyone notice? Why didn't anyone realise I had deflated? I had worked so hard and had no more energy. I needed time off.

I decided to get help. I was grieving a school building, my classroom, and the loss of my best friend, Satty Dub, who died at forty of a heart attack. This period was filled with trauma.

I was referred to a neurologist, who assured me of a full recovery, though it would be slow. My brain had shut down. I could feel my brain trying to remember memories. I suffered from head explosions, insomnia and psychosis. The screams grew louder and louder.

The worst part was that nobody on my team recognised the dangers I faced. Who gives up their maternity for Ofsted? Who sacrifices evenings and weekends for Ofsted? It was me. Chaos consumed my brain and I didn't know I had resigned. My body needed to escape. I wish someone had come to see me that d ay. I wish my headteacher, who was also my friend, had recognised that I was unwell. I masked it well, telling everyone I was going for a promotion while I was struggling. Certain individuals made it difficult and my brain shut down. The trauma lasted three years. I heard doors slamming in my head and locked myself out of the school I loved. I lost all my friendships and couldn't remember being there. The memory returned three years later. I remembered running around the hall shouting, "I'm leaving!"

I looked toward the door, and my brain told me to run. I gathered my things and ran out as if the building were on fire. I needed to go.

At home, silence filled the air. I left the school building and my class. I waited two years and lasted one month. What had I done?

Nothing made sense. I went to the new school as if I had never been anywhere else. I was mentally exhausted and diagnosed with PTSD, which may have started as postnatal depression. I couldn't believe it. I had worked so hard and then locked myself out.

# CHAPTER SEVEN

# Microaggressions

"When someone shows you who they are, believe them the first time."

—Maya Angelou

I had always cherished my dream of being a teacher. Growing up in London, I had seen the impact that dedicated educators could have on a student's life. I pursued my degree in education with unwavering determination and graduated from a top university.

On my first day at the school in Oxfordshire, I arrived early to set up my Year 5 classroom. The room was a blend of colourful posters, educational materials, and a warm, inviting atmosphere I had carefully prepared. However, my enthusiasm was soon met with a series of subtle yet unsettling remarks.

"You're not what I expected," remarked an older teacher, as she looked me up and down. "I thought you'd be … more local."

"Well, I did grow up in London," I responded with a polite smile. "But I'm excited to bring my experiences here."

In the staffroom, I often felt out of place. Conversations would shift or go silent when I entered, and my attempts to join in were met with polite indifference. During staff meetings, my suggestions were frequently overlooked, and I could sense the unspoken doubts about my abilities.

Despite these challenges, I remained resolute. I poured my energy into my teaching, and my students quickly came to appreciate my engaging methods and genuine care. My classroom became a place of vibrant learning and mutual respect.

My innovative teaching techniques soon drew the attention of the headteacher. He was particularly impressed with how I managed to make difficult concepts in mathematics accessible to all my students. When a vacancy for the lead mathematics coordinator arose, I was an obvious choice.

In the meeting where the promotion was announced, I could feel the tension in the room. The headteacher praised my achievements and appointed me to the new role, but the reception from my colleagues was lukewarm at best. The parent's expression barely masked her disapproval.

"Well, let's see how this new approach works out," she said, her tone dripping with scepticism.

I, undeterred, embraced my new responsibilities. I introduced creative problem-solving exercises and organised after-school study groups, leading to a noticeable improvement in students' performance. My success, however, did little to quell the underlying prejudice among some of my peers.

As I settled into my role as the lead mathematics coordinator, I encountered a new challenge in the form of a particularly difficult parent.

From their first interaction, it was clear that he had issues with me, though he cloaked his disdain in a veneer of concern.

"I'm very concerned about the new maths curriculum," the parent began during a parent-teacher meeting. His tone was polite but laced with condescension. "My son, says that your methods are … unconventional."

"Thank you for sharing your concerns," I replied calmly. "I've found that these methods help students understand the material more deeply and improve their critical thinking skills."

The parent's visits became frequent, each one more hostile than the last. He questioned my every decision, often hinting that my background made me unfit to teach his son.

"I just don't see how someone from your … background can understand what our children need," he said one day, his mask of politeness slipping.

I felt a surge of anger but remained composed. "I assure you, that I am fully qualified and committed to providing the best education for all my students."

Despite his continuous efforts to undermine me, the results spoke for themselves. His grades improved, and he began to show a genuine interest in mathematics. However, this did little to change attitude.

One evening after another tense meeting, I confided in the headteacher. "It's frustrating, dealing with these constant attacks. I know I'm making a difference, but sometimes it feels like it's never enough."

He looked at me with sympathy and respect. "You're doing an incredible job. The progress your students are making is remarkable. Unfortunately, some people are slow to change their views, but your dedication and success are undeniable. Keep doing what you're doing."

Buoyed by his support, I continued to focus on my students, proving through my tireless efforts and outstanding results that I was every bit as capable as my counterparts. I knew that change would come slowly, but I remained steadfast, determined to show that excellence knows no cultural or racial boundaries.

It is hard to believe that in 2024, racism and microaggressions still exist. From the moment I step foot into the building, I am looked up and down and automatically it is assumed I am uneducated and probably an unqualified teacher who can't speak English very well.

I once worked in a school where I had to get the governors involved because parents would not stop complaining about my methods. I had to have an hour-long meeting to explain to a parent where 'I had come from' and my educational background. They were pleasantly surprised when I mentioned I had qualified in 2004 and was actually teaching in London before moving to the countryside.

It was quite frustrating that I did exactly the same as my White counterparts but it was a problem when it was an Asian person doing the job.

I once worked in a school where anything and everything was a problem because I was the 'brown girl.' Each and every day, I would walk into the building, and the headteacher would share another complaint. If a White counterpart did it, there was no problem.

It became pretty unbearable, and soon I decided that quitting was the best protocol. It was hard to be in a school where I was not accepted.

I am looking forward to moving back to London, where being brown is not only accepted but is normal.

# CHAPTER EIGHT

# I don't want to teach anymore

'I have learnt that making a living is not the same as making a life.'

—Mary Angelou

A day in December 2021, something was off. I was dragging my feet into work and everything felt distant and disjointed. I remember doing a maths booster group but I couldn't concentrate. I blinked hard, trying to refocus. My headteacher came into my classroom and stood staring at me. There was discomfort in the air. Suddenly, a shrill, disembodied voice echoed through the classroom, calling my name repeatedly. I looked around, my eyes scanning the room for any sign of somebody ese, but all I saw were confused and concerned faces of my students. The voice grew louder, more insistent, and then, as if on cue, the yellow flashing lights began.

They were everywhere, pulsating from the walls, the floor, even my students seemed to be enveloped in the bright, dizzying flashes. My heart raced; I clutched the edge of my desk, trying to steady myself. But the combination of voices and lights was too much. Panic overtook my, and without thinking, I bolted from the classroom, leaving behind my bewildered students and colleagues.

Outside, the cool air hit my face like a splash of water, grounding me momentarily. I stumbled to the school office, mumbling something incoherent to the secretary before collapsing into a chair. With a whirlwind of confusion and fear, I went home.

In the weeks that followed, I underwent numerous medical evaluations. The diagnosis was clear: severe burnout and stress-induced hallucinations. The chaos around me became chaos in my head and soon I became paranoid, impulsive and irrational. I applied for a new job, hoping a change of environment might help me heal.

I never realised I was leaving my old school for good. I was offered the position of KS2 Leader and I accepted without actually thinking of the consequences. Unfortunately, burnout lingered and in the summer term I was signed off with amnesia.

My memory began to falter. I would forget meeting, lose track of conversations and often find myself standing in a room unable to remember I was there. I convinced myself I was never going to teach again.

Slowly the summer turned to autumn and I began to find my footing again. Teaching was in my blood, and I couldn't stay away forever, However, returning to a traditional classroom setting was out of the question. Instead, I started tutoring children with special needs in their homes. It was a far cry from the structured environment of a school but it offered me the flexibility I needed.

I vividly remember my first day tutoring. I sat across from a teenager named Max, who was still in his pyjamas, clearly uninterested in the lesson I had prepared. I felt a pang of despair, thinking I had hit rock bottom. Here I was, a recently qualified headteacher, reduced to a coaxing a sullen teenager to do his maths homework.

But as the days passed, I found myself a new rhythm. I connected with Max in ways I hadn't expected, discovering a profound sense of fulfilment in the one-to-one interactions. The work was challenging but deeply rewarding, and slowly, my confidence began to rebuild.

Bolstered by the success as a tutor, I decided to take on a new challenge. I applied for a position as a Special Educational Needs Disabilities Coordinator (SENDCo). It was a role that combined my passion for teaching with my desire to make a difference in the lives of children with special needs.

However, my tenure as a SENDCo was fraught with difficulties. I faced microaggressions from colleagues who doubted my abilities and questioned my decisions. The constant undermining wore me down, and after a particularly harsh confrontation, I decided to quit. It was a painful decision but I knew I couldn't stay in an environment that was detrimental to my well-being.

Life after quitting was a series of unexpected turns. I felt adrift, unsure of the next step. The career I had dedicated to my life seemed to have turned its back on me. In this period of uncertainty, I discovered new aspects of myself. I took up writing, a hobby I had long neglected, and found solace in creating art.

As the months passed, I realised that my journey wasn't over. I had weathered storms that would have broken many, and in doing so, she had uncovered a resilience I hadn't known I possessed. Teaching had been my identity for so long, but it wasn't the entirety of who I was.

In time, I found my way back to education but on my own terms. I became an advocate for mental health awareness using my experiences to help others navigate the challenges I faced. I started writing and sharing my story with a wider audience and found a new purpose in empowering others.

At the time, I was diagnosed with post-traumatic stress disorder. I could hear my brain 'poppin.' I could hear the files being re-organised and the headaches became severe. I continued working but tiredness truly took over my body. I would make mistakes and need so much sleep. I could feel my body so drained from mental exhaustion and it took over two years to feel any sense of normality. I could hear voices…I could hear them… 'You need to do this...' 'She said this...' 'She said that...' 'Who do you think you are!' Pop...Pop...POP!

My journey was one of trails and tribulations, but also growth and rediscovery, I had thought I was lost, but in truth, I was on the path to finding myself.

# CHAPTER NINE

# Therapy

'You may encounter many defeats but you must not be defeated.'

—Maya Angelou

I continuously had therapy from January 2022 onwards. This chapter is dedicated to my therapist.

It was Friday, January 14, 2022. My best friend Satty called me in the evening and we sat on the phone for nearly two hours. He was so proud of himself and his achievements. We giggled about life, the plans for the future and the joy that he brings to us all.

There are some people who come into our lives who bring light so great that even after they have gone that light remains. Satty was one of those people—he bought light, joy and a huge amount of love for the people in his life. I met Satty over twenty years ago and from the very beginning of our relationship, he gave me so much time and so much love.

When we first met, we would spend so much time at his favourite restaurant on the Broadway, Bombay 177, because we shared a massive love for food. We would spend hours on the phone because conversations never came to an end. One evening, he called and said, 'Sheetal, I want you in my life forever. Will you be my little sister and tie a Rakhi on me?'

From then, we had a special bond. He was always very protective, very caring, and always around through the good times and the bad. When he came back from Australia, the first thing he did was put his arm out and say, 'Sorry I was so far; you can tie all the Rakhi's you missed on me now!' The occasion was always so important to him. He truly was the kindest person to ever enter my life, and we shared so many happy moments.

Satty was very good at connecting people, and one day he said, 'You need to hang out with Shevell. We would be such a great team!' He was so right. From that moment, it was the three of us and he named us the SSS Crew. We grew up and did so much together, from partying in Ealing to cookery classes. He had so much patience and was always such a perfectionist. We would be starving and he would be pretending to be a five-star chef, taking his time plating carefully. He would always say presentation is important—you can't rush it. As life went on and we became mums, he adapted to our lives and became the greatest uncle to our children. Like he did with us, he gave them so much time, love, and care. He would always say, 'They are my children too!' I would like to share my last conversation with Satty, which took place two days before he passed. We spoke for hours and we laughed. He kept saying he felt old because he was sitting at home on a Friday night. What I can tell you is that there were lots of things he was truly happy about and lots that made him proud. He was proud of his recent achievements, and he truly made the most of every moment. He was so happy he had made it to forty.

The final thing I would like to share is a poem, because Satty would never want to see anyone sad, and if he could say anything, this would be the closest.

Don't remember me with sadness,
Don't remember me with tears,
Remember all the laughter,
We've shared throughout the years.
Now I am contented,
That my life it was worthwhile,
Knowing that I passed along the way,
I made somebody smile.
When you are walking down the street,
And you've got me on your mind,
I'm walking in your footsteps,
Only half a step behind.
So please don't be unhappy,
Just because I'm out of sight.
Remember that I am with you,
Each morning, noon, and night.'

I decided to go into therapy because I'd lost myself and my world. In every area of my life post-pandemic, I was struggling. I'd waited two years to return to work and lost the school that I adored after one month of returning. I was sitting at a new school completely exhausted; my marriage was suffering; my youngest boy was constantly in the hospital, and then I lost my best friend.

The decision to go into therapy was not an easy one. For months, I had managed to convince myself that I could handle my emotions, burying the pain beneath layers of busyness and distractions. But as time passed, the weight of unresolved trauma began to seep through the cracks, manifesting in ways I could no longer ignore.

I remember the first session vividly. I strolled to Sarah's lodge, my heart pounding with a mix of anxiety and scepticism. The room was calm, almost too calm, with soft lighting and white walls. It felt like a sanctuary, a stark contrast to the chaos swirling within me.

Sarah greeted me with a warm smile and an inviting presence. She was a woman with kind eyes that seemed to see right through the façade I had carefully constructed. I took a seat on the comfortable couch, feeling like an exposed nerve, raw and vulnerable.

Sarah encouraged me to start with whatever I felt comfortable sharing. I found myself talking about Satty and the shock I was feeling, how I mentally lost myself and was diagnosed with trauma and amnesia and the recent events that had brought me to the brink of despair. Each word felt like a release, a small step toward understanding the labyrinth of my psyche.

One of the most profound benefits of therapy was the development of self-awareness. As I delved deeper into my past and my emotions, I began to recognise patterns in my behaviour and thought processes. I realised how much of my life had been dictated by fear and avoidance. Sarah helped me see that many of my reactions were rooted in unresolved trauma. This insight was like a revelation, shedding light on aspects of myself that I had never fully understood.

Another significant aspect of therapy was learning to practise self-compassion and forgiving myself. I had to remember that the psychological stressors resulted in my actions and I had a mental breakdown. No one else suffered auditory hallucinations or post-traumatic stress disorder. No one else suffered from anxiety and panic attacks. No one else suffered a mental breakdown. Sarah introduced me to the concept of self-compassion, teaching me to treat myself with the same kindness and understanding I would offer a friend. It allowed me to forgive myself, to acknowledge my imperfections without judgment, and to embrace the idea that it was okay to not have all the answers.

Therapy also provided me with practical tools to manage my anxiety and stress. Through various techniques, such as mindfulness and cognitive-behaviour strategies, I learned how to ground myself in the present moment and challenge negative thought patterns. These tools became invaluable in my daily life, helping me navigate challenges with a sense of calm and resilience that I had previously lacked. I decided to join the gym to help with my recovery. It was important that my mind and body re-aligned. Years had passed, but my brain was stuck in the past. I didn't know what I was doing until it was done. I couldn't go back to the past and fix what needed fixing. I couldn't put my things back into my classroom and tell my headteacher that I wasn't well. I was fragile and broken. You know I would never leave! I went for the interview because you said, 'I don't need you here!' All the remarks hurt. I became so obsessed with what people would say about me. I lost myself and ran.

As I became more attuned to my own needs and emotions, I also became more empathetic and understanding toward others. I learned to set healthy boundaries and to engage in relationships from a place of authenticity rather than fear. This shift had a profound impact on my connections with friends and family, fostering deeper and more meaningful bonds.

Looking back, I see therapy as a pivotal turning point in my life. It was a journey inward, one that required courage and vulnerability but ultimately led to profound healing and growth. The process was not linear. There were setbacks and moments of doubt. But with each session, I moved closer to a version of myself that felt whole and authentic.

In the sanctuary of Dr Grace's office, I found a safe space to unravel the complexities of my mind and heart. Therapy was not a cure-all. It did not erase the past or eliminate pain. But it provided me with the tools to navigate my emotions with grace and resilience, to understand myself on a deeper level and to approach life with a renewed sense of hope and possibility.

As I continue on this journey, I carry with me the lessons learned in therapy. They serve as a foundation, a guiding light in times of darkness. I am not defined by my past, nor am I limited by my fears. I am a work in progress, continually evolving, and for the first time in a long time, I am at peace with that.

# CHAPTER TEN

# Oxfordshire Mind, Banbury, Women's Support Group

'You may shoot me with your words, you may cut me with your eyes, you may kill me with your hatefulness but still, like air, I'll rise!'

—Maya Angelou

Life was challenging; my marriage was failing, and I was scared about the future. The thought of raising my two little boys on my own and possibly having a relapse haunted me. How I left the school where I was meant to be weighed heavily on me, so I decided to seek further help.

I met with a Social Prescribing Wellbeing Worker in Primary Care, who suggested visiting a women's support group by Oxfordshire Mind in Banbury.

On Tuesday, May 28, 2024, I visited the group and was warmly welcomed. The facilitators gave me a tour and I loved the room. It had a sense of warmth with beautiful artwork displayed on the walls, art for sale, jewellery made by volunteers, a portable heater by my table, and refreshments.

I decided to try some diamond art, and to my surprise, I thoroughly enjoyed it. For the next hour and a half, I was absorbed in picking up little gems and placing them on a sticky board to create a floral heart. Concentrating on each gem, in shades of pink, purple, yellow, and orange, was very calming and therapeutic.

I shared my story and felt fortunate to do so. Selfishly, I was glad that the worst was over, as many others had faced far worse experiences. Time went by as I continued the diamond art, and for the first time in a long time, I heard nothing. No whispers in my ears, no screams in my head. Just silence. I felt like I could think clearly, breathe, and begin to process the last few years and what was coming next.

For anyone in need, there are so many resources available. Talking therapies, Oxfordshire Mind women's support group, counselling, art therapy—the list is endless. Please don't be afraid to seek help; you can become part of a supportive community, starting with visiting your GP.

Mental Health Services—Some Examples

Your GP: The first step
Helplines:

- Mind Infoline: 0300 123 3393
- The Legal Line: 0300 466 6463
- The Samaritans: 116 123

Local Resources:

- Oxfordshire Sexual Abuse and Rape Crisis Centre: 01865 725 311
- Talking Space Therapy
- Cruse Bereavement Care Oxfordshire: 01865 245 398
- The Listening Centre: 01865 794 794
- Oxford Mindfulness Centre: 01865 613 157

## CHAPTER ELEVEN

# Spiritual Healing

"What you're supposed to do when you don't like a thing is change it. If you can't change it, change the way you think about it. Don't complain."

—Maya Angelou

I spent days, weeks, even months trying to change a single moment in time. Exhausted beyond measure, I was asked to write my resignation. So tired and unaware of my actions, I couldn't foresee the consequences that would follow. Struggling to rejoin society, my mind was stuck in the past while my body moved on. Time continued but my memory began to fade, leading to insomnia and an episode of psychosis. Night after night, I heard screams and longed for peaceful sleep. Overwhelmed by the demands of everyone around me, I was utterly drained.

Desperate, I called my father and confided in him. He asked me to trust him and come to a church, so I did. He was deeply worried. I had reached a point where I was ready to end my life. Joy had vanished, my best friend had died and I felt utterly lost. Despite having much to be happy about, none of it brought me joy. Suffering from amnesia, I feared I wouldn't see my two young boys grow up or remember them at all.

I went to a church in Datchet, where the priest was a spiritual healer. He held weekly gatherings to recite passages from the Bible and spread God's Word. His deep empathy and compassion allowed him to connect with and understand the emotions of those he helped. He maintained a calm, grounded presence, creating a peaceful and healing atmosphere.

The priest asked me to relax, and I suddenly fell to the floor. I heard him reciting Bible verses and praying. Then I felt a heat emanating from my head; my eyes flickered, and my legs shook. I felt very, very cold.

The people around him used instruments to create vibrations that promote relaxation and healing. This sound healing aims to restore harmony and balance within the body and mind.

At that moment, I had a vision: Jesus came to me. Wearing a white robe with a blinding light behind him, he said, "You will be all right." I may have been numb, but it felt like he took my worries away. I woke up feeling different. For the first time in many days, I could sleep, eat and enjoy the laughter around me. I felt embraced and accepted, with a sense of clarity and purpose. All doubts vanished, replaced by a profound connection and love with God. I felt fortunate to be given another chance.

Experiencing God in a vision was a true spiritual insight. I felt lifted and loved, overwhelmed by a deep sense of knowing. Guided and comforted, this life-altering event instilled in me a deep sense of purpose and faith. The vision remains vivid and impactful, giving me strength to carry on through hardships. It profoundly shaped my understanding of the divine and my place in the universe.

I believe that the heavenly light was a vision of Jesus, symbolising his divine nature. The soft, glowing light was bright and powerful, illuminating everything. Jesus stood with open arms, inviting and welcoming, symbolising love, grace, and salvation. His presence was calming, filled with divine love and protection. The vision inspired me, filling me with purpose, hope, and a deeper connection.

Seeing Jesus in a dream symbolises hope and clarity, leading to a more devout, purpose-driven life. Since the vision, I have reflected on my life, emotions and spiritual state to understand its significance. Dreaming of Jesus represents a subconscious desire for protection, guidance, or validation, helping the mind process deep-seated fears, hopes, and aspirations. Jesus provides compassion, forgiveness, and wisdom, guiding me through challenges and obstacles. This vision has led to personal transformation, moving me toward greater spiritual and emotional health.

I have taken specific steps in my personal, spiritual and communal life, such as helping others, seeking forgiveness and spreading kindness. I feel like I'm making better choices and following a more righteous path. This experience has encouraged me to deepen my spiritual practices and realign my life with my values and beliefs. It has provided peace and comfort during distressful times, offering reassurance and support. Seeing Jesus in a dream affirms his divine presence and my faith, reminding me that I am not alone and that a higher power watches over me.

# CHAPTER TWELVE

# Whispers of Destiny—Meeting a Medium

'Stand up straight and realise who you are, that you tower over your circumstances.'

—Maya Angelou

I had always taken an interest in the supernatural. Growing up in a bustling city before moving to the relaxing countryside, my life was rooted in the tangible and the concrete. But in desperation, I wanted to seek out the unexplainable. So, I found myself standing at the door of a modest, ivy-covered cottage. Its wooden sign was swaying in the breeze: "Hanson—Medium and Spiritual Guide."

Taking a deep breath, I pushed open the creaky door and stepped inside. The interior was dimly lit, a faint scent of incense lingering in the air. Shelves lined with crystals, tarot cards and ancient books surrounded a small table draped in rich, purple velvet. Seated behind the table was a woman with silver-streaked hair and piercing blue eyes that seemed to look right through me.

"Welcome, Sheetal." Hanson greeted me with a warm smile. "I've been expecting you."

I felt a shiver run down my spine.

Hanson nodded, gesturing for me to take a seat. "Sit, my dear. The spirits have much to tell you."

Hesitant but curious, I sat down. Hanson took my hands, and I closed my eyes for a moment, as if listening to an unseen force. When I opened them again, my gaze was intense.

"You are writing a book," she began, her voice soft but assured. "A book that will touch many lives."

My eyes widened. "How did you—"

Hanson held up a hand. "The spirits speak, my dear. They tell me you have been through immense mental challenges, trials that would have broken many. But you endured because you were destined to help others."

A lump formed in my throat. I had never shared my struggles with anyone outside my immediate circle. "Why me?" I whispered.

"You are an earth angel," Hanson said, her eyes gleaming with a knowing light. "You have walked this Earth before, and you have returned to aid those around you. Your book is just the beginning. It will be a success and you are destined to write many more."

The weight of Hanson's words hung in the air, heavy yet uplifting. I felt a strange mix of emotions: disbelief, hope, and a deep-seated sense of purpose.

Hanson continued, her tone unwavering. "I see a city in your future. You are moving there soon, guided by forces beyond your control. It is where you are meant to be. The countryside was never your true home; it was merely a stop along your journey. The city is where your destiny unfolds."

My heart raced. The idea of moving had been circling my mind for months, but I had yet to decide. "But why? Why do I need to go to the city?"

"Because the energies are aligning to place you where you can have the most impact," Hanson explained. "You were never meant to stay here. The forces are ensuring that you find your path to the city, where you will thrive and fulfil your destiny."

I felt a strange sense of clarity, as if puzzle pieces were finally falling into place. "What do I need to do to protect myself on this journey?" I asked.

Hanson smiled gently, releasing my hands and reaching for a small pouch. "Crystals," she said, pulling out a few sparkling stones. "Carry these with you. Amethyst for protection, rose quartz for love and healing, and citrine for success. They will shield you from negative energies."

I took the crystals, their cool weight grounding me. "Thank you," I murmured.

"And remember," Hanson added, "you have a guardian angel watching over you. You are never alone, no matter how daunting the path ahead may seem."

Tears welled up in my eyes. The medium's words resonated deeply, offering a sense of comfort and direction I hadn't realised I had needed. I rose to my feet, clutching the crystals tightly.

"Thank you, Hanson," I said, my voice steady. "You've given me a lot to think about."

Hanson nodded, her expression serene. "Trust in the journey, Sheetal. You are exactly where you need to be, and the future holds great things for you."

As I stepped out of the cottage and into the sunlight, I felt a newfound sense of purpose. The road ahead was still uncertain, but for the first time in a long while, I felt ready to embrace it. My destiny awaited, and I was prepared to meet it head-on, guided by the whispers of spirits and the light of my guardian angel.

On my road to recovery, I did speak to a medium—online though. I was in awe of her. I was stunned every time she picked a card from the tarot pack. I purposely didn't tell her about my life: she mentioned she saw me writing a book, and honestly, I could have stomped to the floor. Really? Everything above is what she said: she mentioned that I was meant to be writing, and everything that happened was supposed to happen! I had many mental challenges, and she told me that each and every one happened so that I could be of use to others. She said I never belonged in the countryside: I always was and always will be a city girl!

## CHAPTER THIRTEEN

# Hypnotherapy

"Nothing will work unless you do."

—Maya Angelou

The classroom was chaos. The sound of thirty voices talking at once, the scrape of chairs against linoleum, the constant beeping of the old fluorescent lights overhead—these were the sounds that had become the soundtrack to my days. But today, it was all too much.

I had been a teacher for twenty years. I had started my career full of passion and idealism, determined to make a difference in the lives of my students. But over time, the system had worn me down. The endless pressure, the lack of resources, the constant demands from administration, and the growing list of students with complex needs—it all weighed heavily on me. The pressure to get all pupils through the SATS, leading a school inspection, and adults acting immaturely was all too much.

I stood at the front of the room, trying to get my students' attention. "All right, everyone, let's settle down and get started on our maths lesson," I called out, forcing a smile. But my voice was drowned out by the chatter and the clattering.

"Mrs Smith, can I go to the bathroom?" one student shouted.

"Mrs Smith, I forgot my homework," another said.

"Mrs Smith, can you help me with this?" came a third voice.

I felt a familiar tightness in my chest, a sensation that had been growing stronger each day. I felt like I was being crushed under an invisible weight. My hands began to shake, and I gripped the edge of my desk to steady myself.

"Mrs Smith?" a voice broke through the din, sounding concerned. It was Jamie, one of my more perceptive students.

I tried to respond, but the words stuck in my throat. The room started to blur, and I felt a wave of dizziness wash over me. I couldn't do this anymore. I couldn't pretend that everything was fine.

Without another word, I turned and walked out of the classroom. The noise of the students followed me into the hallway, but it was quickly muffled by the sound of my own heartbeat pounding in my ears. I made my way to the staff bathroom, locked the door behind me, and sank to the floor, tears streaming down my face.

I didn't know how long I sat there sobbing, but eventually the tears stopped, leaving me feeling hollow and exhausted. I knew I needed help. I couldn't keep going like this.

A week later, I found myself sitting in the waiting room of a hypnotherapy clinic. It had been my aunt Pip who had suggested hypnotherapy. I had been sceptical at first, but I was desperate for anything that might help me regain control of my life.

The hypnotherapist said that hypnotherapy was about re-starting the brain and re-framing it. It was about lifting my mood and accepting the trauma. The body would allow for the memories to exist without it affecting my emotions as much as they have.

The therapist, Dr Ray, greeted me warmly and led me into a cozy, softly lit room. There was a comfortable chair in the centre, and soothing music played quietly in the background.

"Sheetal, I'm glad you came," Dr Ray said, sitting down opposite me. "Hypnotherapy can be a powerful tool for reframing negative thoughts and emotions. Are you ready to begin?"

I nodded, feeling a flicker of hope for the first time in a long while. I followed Dr Ray's instructions, focusing on my breathing and allowing myself to relax. Slowly, I felt myself sinking into a deep, tranquil state.

"Sheetal"—Dr. Raja's voice was gentle but firm—"I want you to imagine a place where you feel completely safe and at peace. Can you picture that place?"

I nodded again, my mind conjuring up an image of a secluded beach I had visited years ago. I could hear the sound of the waves and feel the warmth of the sun on my skin.

"In this place, you are free from all worries and stress," Dr Ray continued. "Now, I want you to imagine that you are holding a heavy backpack. This backpack contains all the burdens and negative thoughts that have been weighing you down. Can you see it?"

I imagined the backpack, feeling its weight pressing down on my shoulders.

"Now Sheetal, I want you to take that backpack off and set it down. Feel the weight lifting from your shoulders."

As I followed the instructions, I felt an incredible sense of relief. It was as if a physical burden had been removed from my body.

"Good," Dr. Raja said. "Now, I want you to repeat these affirmations after me: I am strong. I am capable. I am worthy of peace and happiness."

I repeated the words, and with each repetition, I felt a little stronger, a little more at peace.

Over the next few weeks, I continued my hypnotherapy sessions with Dr Ray. Each session helped me release more of the negative thoughts and emotions that had been holding me back. I learned techniques to manage my stress and began to reframe my thoughts in a more positive light.

In the classroom, I started to notice a difference. I was more patient with my students, more compassionate with myself. I set boundaries and made time for my self-care. I rediscovered the joy in teaching, focusing on the small victories and the connections I made with my students.

One day as I was wrapping up a lesson, Jamie approached me with a smile. "Mrs Smith, you seem different," he said. "Happier."

I smiled back, feeling a warmth in my heart. "Thank you, Jamie. I am happier."

As I watched my students file out of the classroom, I felt a renewed sense of purpose. I knew that the road ahead would still have its challenges but I was ready to face them. I was stronger now, more resilient. I had found my way back to myself and was ready to embrace the future with hope and optimism.

## CHAPTER FOURTEEN

# Preparing for an Ofsted Inspection

'Stand up straight and realise who you are, that you tower over your circumstances.'

—Maya Angelou

The following chapters are a series of blogs I wrote for *Nexus Education* and *RISE* magazine. I hope you find them useful.

In 2023, I had the fortunate experience of shadowing the Senior South-East HMI team on Ofsted inspections. The shadow programme was an opportunity for future leaders, in particular from ethnic minorities, to have an insight to inspections and encourage under-represented people to join the Ofsted workforce.

First of all, Ofsted inspectors follow the Inspection Handbook as if it was their Bible. If you are worried about inspections and want to know what the inspections will be on, read it!

Reading is the main priority in inspections. It is important to know that developing a reading culture is important because pupils can then access all areas of the curriculum. It's not just about asking them to read a book at home; it is about having a love for reading. Promote a love of reading through author visits, school reading events, reading certificates, and sharing book titles and covers. It is about investing in a programme that allows all pupils to read without falling behind their peers.

Nexus Education: Preparing for an Ofsted Deep Dive in Reading

Preparing for a Deep Dive in Reading

The new Education Inspection Framework includes a mandatory reading deep dive where inspectors will look at the seven aspects of early reading (paragraph 298 of the school inspection handbook). Inspectors will focus on how well pupils are taught to read as a main inspection activity, as it is important for pupils to learn how to read fluently as quickly as possible; after all, 'fluent readers are able to read and gain knowledge for themselves.'

Department for Education English Hubs

Before looking at the deep dive in reading, it is important to know that there are thirty-four Department for Education English Hubs able to provide support for excellent teaching in phonics and early language. They focus on supporting the slowest progress children in Reception and Year 1 through action planning, reading audits, funding for training, and support and access to a literacy specialist.

Letters and Sounds 2007

The 2007 Letters and Sounds Framework is no longer sufficient to follow, as it is not a full programme that sets out in detail how phonics should be taught on a week-by-week basis. It is recommended that schools use a validated Systematic Synthetic Phonics teaching programme (SSP), as it has been designed by experts in the field and has all the relevant resources, reading books, and high-quality training that ensure an approach that is 'rigorous and used with fidelity.'

Deep Dive in Reading

- All staff should be trained in the school's chosen phonics programme, and pupils should be taught direct, focused phonics from the beginning of Reception and Key Stage 1 every day.
- If pupils fall behind the programme, leaders should ensure that extra practice throughout the day is provided so that they can 'keep up' rather than 'catch up.'
- All resources used should match the phonics programme and be used consistently in all phases.
- Decodable books are organised in the given sequence in their chosen SSP programme—pupils should not be asked to read books that require them to guess words or deduce meanings from pictures, grammar, clues, etc.
- Pupils from KS1 and KS2 (Year 3) will be asked to read. Inspectors will concentrate on the lowest 20 per cent and will want to know if a school has a team of expert reading teachers: if the slowest progress readers in key stage 2 can read age-appropriate unseen books with fluency.
- The Reading Leader provides high-quality CPD and ensures that all new staff are trained in the programme.
- Parents are well-informed and books/phonics folders are taken home.

Reading in Key Stage Two

All pupils should pass the phonics screening and be able to read before starting Year 3. If pupils are still learning to read in Key Stage Two, they should remain on the school's chosen phonics programme. As an English Leader, it is important to observe and monitor the impact of any reading interventions across the school. In some cases, pupils may be able to read but struggle with comprehension. The Education Endowment Foundation provides information on improving reading in Key Stage Two—all of which have a high impact and a low cost to schools. For example, explicitly teaching reading strategies has proven to have an impact on pupils by at least six months.

Developing a Reading Culture

Inspectors will be asking pupils about their reading and assessing whether the school has been able to develop a love for reading. Ensure there is a timetabled slot for reading for pleasure, story-time in all phases, and a reading corner in every classroom. Reading should be promoted through the use of the library, author visits, and reading events. Many schools ensure that pupils have a decodable reading book and a book from the library (reading book for pleasure) to take home to share with their parents.

In the early years and KS1, stories, rhymes, songs, and poems should be shared regularly, and inspectors will ask about what has been chosen to develop children's vocabulary. Encouraging children in KS2 to read widely and research will develop their vocabulary—you may want to think about book recommendations/book lists and a text-based curriculum where books are chosen from the reading plagues, different cultures, and texts that show underrepresented groups. Pupils should also have access to a range of poetry: choral, classic, etc.

Engaging Parents

Not all parents have the time to visit the school for a workshop on reading, but keeping reading high profile is important, and providing a newsletter can be extremely useful. In the past, I have written a monthly newsletter to parents about our school's chosen phonics programme, how they can support their child with reading at home, reading strategies, and much more. It has been a useful way to communicate the importance of reading and ensuring that pupils read at home every day.

Monitoring

As an English Leader, it is important to 'drop-in' to classrooms and ensure there is consistency between Reception and Key Stage One. It is important to ensure that a tracking system is in place so that pupils who have fallen behind have the opportunity for extra lessons to 'keep-up.' It is also important to ensure that all teaching assistants are trained in the programme and that all staff are consistent in their approach. Inspectors will want to see that the school has made reading a priority and ensures every child learns to read in their school.

Lastly, the deep dive in reading is a team effort. It is important that all leaders and all staff work together to ensure that every child in their school is able to read despite their ability or background.

# CHAPTER FIFTEEN

# Busting the Ofsted Myths!

'Do the best you can until you know better, then, when you know better, do better!'

—Maya Angelou

The death of Ruth Perry (previous Headteacher of Caversham PriMaya School) sparked rage and concerns over Ofsted inspections.

According to the BBC News, an inquest ruled that an Ofsted inspection "contributed" to the death of headteacher Ruth Perry. The inspection "lacked fairness, respect and sensitivity" and was at times "rude and intimidating," senior coroner Heidi Connor said.

There is great pressure on senior leaders and headteachers to ensure that a 'good' or 'outstanding' grade is awarded. Whilst pupil progress and attainment are the key objectives, it is not always easy to keep up with government changes and ensure all members of staff are compliant. Many senior leaders are burnt out and suffering mental health issues.

Whilst I am not an expert, I hope this article may bring a little ease, as there are many myths. I was recently selected to join the Ofsted Future Leaders Programme, which provided the opportunity to have training on the Education Inspection Framework and shadow senior HMI on inspections.

Busting Myth Number 1: Paperwork

There is no need to do additional paperwork. I was the senior leader who spent hours through the night preparing folders. They will not be opened! What do you need?

- A clear progression map showing knowledge and skills for each curriculum area.
- An action plan for each subject—showing how learning experiences will improve for children.
- Coverage of National Curriculum objectives.

Busting Myth Number 2: Teaching

Senior leaders can be quite obsessed with everyone having the same teaching style. Ofsted understand that teachers will have different styles; of course, there are some whole school strategies, but overall, they observe pupil behaviour, attitudes, and progress within the lesson and over time.

Busting Myth Number 3: Marking

I have been in schools where I have introduced the Shirley Clarke highlighting marking and in schools were marking is pretty much a stamp at the end of a piece of work. Ofsted do not look for in-depth marking; they want senior leaders to reduce teacher workload. Teachers are not required to write reams of comments if there is no impact—the marking policy should be regularly reviewed.

Busting Myth Number 4: Lesson Planning

It strikes me that experienced teachers are still required to produce daily lesson plans. Ofsted do not look at daily lesson plans. They will require a long-term and medium-term plan that shows the objectives—this is to ensure that the school is meeting the statutory requirements. Curriculum leaders should be able to speak about the curriculum throughout the school.

Busting Myth Number 5: Differentiation

The days of tasks in all lessons needing to be differentiated are gone! Differentiation has now been replaced with 'adaptive teaching.' Teachers should be making adjustments where required: maybe a change of language, using questions, and providing challenging tasks.

Busting Myth Number 6: Fancy Lessons

When planning an Ofsted lesson, do what you always do! There is no need for up-beat, fancy lessons. Ofsted do not have a particular style but are looking to see whether the pupils are learning.

Busting Myth Number 7: Observations

Ofsted do not grade individual lessons—if your school is still doing this, they need to move with the times. Grading is determined by looking at teaching and learning as a whole, triangulation of planning, assessment and data.

Busting Myth Number 8: Evidence for Curriculum Leaders

The inspector will have a discussion with you about your subject. They will want to know 'the picture' across the school. The expectation is that they will see what you have spoken about and that everyone is talking from the same hymn sheet: pupils will say the same, teachers say the same, and lessons show evidence of impact on learning.

Busting Myth number 9: Schemes of Work

I have heard of schools that purchase schemes of work and then ask teachers not to use the materials. Having a scheme of work ensures that there is consistency between year groups; it reduces teacher workload and ensures that pupils make good progress.

Busting Myth Number 10: Reading

Reading is a key priority; it is important that all pupils have access to high-quality literature. Having a validated phonics programme is important, and there should be consistency between Reception and Year 1.

There are no hidden secrets; the Education Inspection Framework is published online and is the Ofsted Bible. Of course, there are discrepancies between inspectors, and there does need to be some change, especially as senior leaders are leaving the profession. I am not an expert but I am happy to offer myself to any member of the teaching staff—whether you have a question, need some advice, or want a training session, you can contact me on LinkedIn or Twitter. @smithme / Mesmith

# CHAPTER SIXTEEN

# Being a SENDCo

'Try to be a rainbow in someone's cloud!

—Maya Angelou

Are you a new SENCO?' As a SENCO, you play a central role in ensuring all learners feel included and have the opportunity to fulfil their true potential. The vision must be shared with every leader and with every teacher for a child-centred approach and transformational impact.

Understanding the Role of a SENCO

As a SENCO, you are in a position to inspire inclusive practice to ensure the best possible outcomes for all children and young people. You should familiarise yourself with *The Children and Families Act* (2014) and the SEND Code of Practice (DfE and DoH, 2014).

As well as having a strategic overview of the policy and practices of your setting, time should be given to monitor the provision that is in place for those with SEND in your setting. According to the SEND Code of Practice, the class teacher should remain responsible for working with the child on a daily basis. The SENCO's role is to support the class teacher and teaching assistants with problem-solving and advising on the effective implementation of support.

Key Legislation

- *The Children and Families Act* (2014)
- The SEND Regulations (2014)
- The Special Educational Needs and Disability Code of Practice: 0-25 years (2014)
- *The Equality Act* (2010)
- The United Nations Convention on the Rights of the Child (1989)
- Working Together to Safeguard Children (2018)
- Supporting Pupils at School with Medical Conditions (2017)

The Four Broad Areas of Need

The SEND Code of Practice outlines 'four broad areas of need.' The four broad areas are:

- Communication and Interaction
- Cognition and Learning
- Social, Emotional, and Mental Health
- Sensory and/or Physical

Communication and Interaction

Young people may often require support with speech production and understanding and expressing language. Sometimes the way in which language is used in the classroom and around school may impact their learning.

Cognition and Learning

There are learning difficulties that may be moderate to severe, and there are profound and multiple learning difficulties, as well as specific learning difficulties. Specific learning difficulties encompass a range of conditions: dyslexia, dyscalculia, dyspraxia, or developmental coordination disorder.

Social, Emotional, and Mental Health

Young people may become withdrawn or isolated, or display challenging behaviour. These behaviours may reflect a range of underlying issues, such as anxiety or depression. Young children may also have Attention Deficit Disorder (ADD), Attention Deficit Hyperactive Disorder (ADHD).

Sensory and/or Physical

Young people may have vision impairment, hearing impairment, as well as physical disabilities.

How will you ensure that every teacher is a teacher of SEND so that all our children can reach their full potential?

Establishing High Expectations

Every teacher needs to be very clear about their responsibilities under the Code of Practice. I would share some key sections from the Code and then explore with the staff what this looks like in practice in this school.

This presents a great opportunity to establish clearly that teachers have a responsibility to know about any additional support children might be receiving, the progress they are making during such sessions, and how they relate to their day-to-day classroom teaching. It is also an ideal time to reinforce that all children should have fair and equal access to the class teacher during lessons.

TAs can make a fantastic contribution to children's learning, but teachers must know that, ultimately, they are responsible for the progress of all children in their class. Expert support from TAs should supplement, not replace, the class teacher.

Training and CPD

It is important to identify staff needs and put appropriate training in place.

I would create an audit to find out what skills and knowledge the staff already have and build on this.

Teachers and TAs like to access the training that is most relevant to them based on their existing skill levels, so I would consider preparing a 'menu' of SEND training opportunities that staff can dip into over time. For example, some staff may want training on focusing on supporting children with literacy difficulties, whilst others choose to learn more about social communication difficulties.

Improving Communication

Ensuring teachers are fully involved in planning, tracking, and evaluating the impact of any additional support children are receiving.

Giving teachers and TAs time to explore specific programmes and how they could link these to their daily lessons.

Providing Advice and Information to Teachers

Short information booklets on topics such as speech and language, social communication, and numeracy/ literacy difficulties can outline some of the common difficulties that children might face, accompanied by a list of suggested strategies for teachers to try.

This is a good way of giving teachers access to a toolkit they can use in their classrooms before seeking more specialist support.

The SEND Register

Ensuring the SEND register is up-to-date and shared with staff. Supporting teachers with SEND trackers and ensuring they have resources needed for particular children. Ensuring that staff have the required paperwork (e.g. EHCPs) for children so that they can make reasonable adjustments in order to meet the needs of all pupils with SEND.

The 'Graduated' Approach

- Ensuring that teachers are aware of the 'graduated' approach

Assess: Teacher Responsibilities

Teacher assessment of pupil progress: Are individuals making expected progress? And if not, why not? It could be useful for teachers/teaching assistants to liaise with colleagues. If there is a concern that the young person may have an unidentified SEND, then the SENDCo should be contacted.

Plan: Teacher Responsibilities

To plan inclusive, high-quality teaching to meet the needs of individuals. Use information provided via Individual Education Plans (IEPs) or Pupil Passports. I would ensure that I am available to support teachers and TAs if in doubt.

Do: Teacher Responsibilities

The development of inclusive lessons to meet the needs of identified individuals (e.g., by using "dyslexia-friendly" strategies).

Review: Teacher Responsibilities

Provide feedback in books or through teacher-student conversations or school reports. TAs may also want to make notes in the students' books. At our school, we are piloting a system whereby the TA uses a code to inform the teacher how much support the pupil requires in order to complete a given task.

Websites

According to the University of Roehampton, some useful websites are:

- www.nasen.org.uk
- www.thecommunicationtrust.org.uk
- www.contact.org.uk
- www.autismeducationtrust.org.uk
- www.place2be.org.uk
- www.youngminds.org.uk

# CHAPTER SEVENTEEN

# Indian Women in Education— It Is Time for Justice

"Success is liking yourself, liking what you do, and liking how you do it."

— Maya Angelou

For centuries, Indian women have been at war to be accepted due to gender inequalities, race, and religion. Opportunities for promotion are paused due to stereotypes, and according to the 'School teacher workforce' (Feb, 2021), only 0.8 per cent of heads were Indian and 1.5 per cent given the roles of deputies or assistant heads in UK schools. Me Smith, a senior leader who comes from a supportive Indian family, informs us of what it can be like culturally and highlights the need to educate and promote diversity in our schools today.

Kalpana Chawla once said, 'The path from dreams to success does exist. May you have the vision to find it, the courage to get on it, and the perseverance to follow it.' As the first woman of Indian origin to go to space, Kalpana became one of the greatest inspirational women to Indian girls around the world. Whilst in some families these historical moments by Indian women are celebrated; in others old cultural systems still remain.

For generations, women in the Indian culture have been seen as subservient due to their role as homemakers and carers. Men are seen as superior and better providers; they continue the 'family name' and are expected to make all the important household decisions and rules. Indian girls are seen as a burden, especially as families are expected to pay a dowry when they get married. Still today, it is tradition for the bride's family to give a dowry to the groom and his family—this consists of a large amount of money and, at times, valuable goods. For some families, this is financially impossible. This leads to families disowning their daughters and ensuring they live a 'simple life,' whilst the best possible opportunities are provided for their sons.

It is every girl's right to strive for equality and end bias in our society. Every girl, including Indian girls, has the right to pursue higher education and a dream job and live in a world where their gender or nationality is not a barrier or a burden. Modern Indian girls are perceived to be care-free and irresponsible when in fact they want to be independent and resilient and provide themselves with a better quality of life.

Inequalities remain in Indian society across the UK and in India. In the UK, it is still common when a young woman has a baby girl for relatives to say, 'Better luck next time.' It has gone as far as relatives and friends not congratulating the mother because she has given birth to a daughter. The pressure of 'having a boy' has also meant a rise in sex-selective abortions. I mean, what century are we truly living in? In India (2006, ABC News), 10 million baby girls were killed by their parents due to their gender. Though criminalised, female infanticide is still very common today.

We need to change people's mindsets and educate them on how powerful Indian women can actually be when given the chance. Indian women take the form of many Hindu deities: like Parvati, they represent the continuity of life; like Lakshmi, they are able to bring good fortune and wealth, and like Saraswati, they are able to bring learning, arts, and music. The representation of Indian women needs to change. They are not 'simple-minded' and passive but strong, independent, and equally have dreams and desires.

'We need women who are so strong they can be gentle, so educated they can be humble, so fierce they can be compassionate, so passionate they can be rational, and so disciplined, they can be free,' Kavita Ramadas. There are many women who inspire us all and who have made some of the greatest achievements; we have the right to have a chance to succeed like them despite our gender, race, or status.

We need to do more to support each other and recognise talents and achievements. Too often the achievements of Indian women are dismissed; the status between men and women remains unequal, and they are still fighting a silent battle—not just because of their gender, but their race, religion, and stereotypes too. We need to do more to promote diversity and inclusion and show pupils globally that they can have the opportunities they desire. They need role models that look like them to believe they have the potential to do it too. We need to show strong women from all backgrounds in our day-to-day teaching through our stories, or show historical achievements from around the world and much more.

'Education is a liberating force, and in our age it is also a democratising force, cutting across the barriers of caste and class, smoothing out inequalities imposed by birth and other circumstances,' Indira Gandhi.

# CHAPTER EIGHTEEN

# International Women's Day!

"My mission in life is not merely to survive,
but to thrive; and to do so with some passion, some
compassion, some humor, and some style."

— Maya Angelou

Martin Luther King once said, 'If I cannot do great things, I can do small things in a great way.'

This year for International Women's Day, women all over the globe are hoping to share, inspire, and move toward a gender-equal world that is free of bias, stereotypes, and discrimination. I can't speak for every woman, but I can share my views as a young Asian leader who has been a victim of discrimination. However, every time I have been knocked down, I have come back stronger, and 'like air, I will [continue] to rise.' Mary Angelou

Inspired by Maya Angelou, I decided to #BreakTheBias by making my voice heard. She once said, 'You should be angry. You must not be bitter. Bitterness is like cancer. It eats upon the host. It doesn't do anything to the object of its displeasure. So use that anger. You write it. You paint it. You dance it. You march it. You vote it. You talk it. Never stop talking it.'

There is a lot that angers me, and it starts with stereotypical views on the television that need to change. Why is it that Asian people on television are most likely to have an accent when this is not always the case? Why are they portrayed as not being able to speak English properly? Why are women always completing household chores, whilst men are seen as superior leaders?

Whether the stereotype is women as less competent, simple-minded, and typically only good for the kitchen, or women of colour as incapable of being leaders because they are seen to be submissive or passive—it all needs to change.

Like many, I am tired. I am tired of constantly proving my worth to 'climb up the ladder!'

Yes, I am an Asian woman who has young children, but I am also committed to my profession! We need people to use their intersectional lens and consider whether some women are having it harder than others.

Have you ever asked about the experience of women, especially women of colour, in your organisation? Have you shifted the focus from the story you may be thinking to the actual messages they present to you?

Not so long ago, I sat amongst friends, and we shared similar experiences in educational establishments. Of course, there were common themes:

- First, the Black woman who had spent most of her career being an expert in the teaching of phonics and was also responsible for training others. When numerous opportunities to lead the area

were advertised, she was not once considered for an interview. Surprisingly, she was actually asked to train the person who was appointed.
- Then the Asian woman who had been teaching for over twenty years, who had a wealth of knowledge in her field, but her voice was constantly dismissed because she 'should be adopting certain behaviours' to be accepted.
- Then the young, Asian woman who showed dedication, and despite saying and doing all the right things, her voice was quieted because she was too passionate!
- Then the natural-born leader who inspires others but is hesitant to take the next step because her accent becomes a barrier.
- Then another … it is endless!

It does truly anger me that women, especially women of colour, are being held back due to their race or age or stereotypes that have been unchallenged time and time again.

For aeons, women have been fighting for equal rights, and even today, women are still existing in an unequal world where they are continuously having to battle stereotypes and prove their worth. We want to be in an inclusive world free from gender bias and where diversity is truly celebrated. Inclusive cultures make people feel valued for who they are and what they bring to an establishment. There needs to be a shift in people's mindset so that people are recognised for their talents and achievements. We can empower people by respecting and appreciating what makes them different.

Whether deliberate or unconscious, bias makes it difficult for women to move ahead. It is still common for women to leave the profession to look after the children whilst the men have opportunities to gain more senior roles. We can begin by being responsible for our own thoughts and actions—all day, every day.

We need to #BreakTheBias by actively calling out gender bias, discrimination, and stereotyping each and every time it is seen.

Every time you make your voice heard, you begin a ripple and inspire others to do the same. Then we will all begin to thrive.

## CHAPTER NINETEEN

# The Dual Role—Being a Mum and a Teacher

"You can only become truly accomplished at something you love. Don't make money your goal. Instead pursue the things you love doing and then do them so well that people can't take their eyes off of you."

— Maya Angelou

Balancing the dual roles of being a mum and a teacher is a unique journey filled with challenges, joys, and constant learning. This chapter explores practical strategies and personal stories. I have the joys of raising two young boys: Reuben, age ten, and Fabian, aged three. My life is hectic: fulltime teacher and parent with very little time for myself.

1. Embracing the Dual Identity

Being both a mum and a teacher means wearing two hats simultaneously. Each role brings its own set of responsibilities, emotions, and experiences. Embracing this dual identity involves recognising the strengths each role brings to the other. As a teacher, your maternal instincts can enhance your empathy and understanding toward your students. Conversely, your teaching skills can benefit your parenting approach, helping you to foster a love of learning in your children. Whenever I teach, I imagine my children with me, and that's how I succeed in every lesson.

2. Time Management Strategies

Effective time management is crucial for balancing the demands of teaching and motherhood. Here are some strategies to consider:

- Prioritise Tasks: Use a planner or digital tool to list and prioritise tasks. Separate urgent tasks from those that can wait.
- Set Boundaries: Establish clear boundaries between work and home life. Designate specific times for grading papers, lesson planning, and family activities.
- Delegate: Don't hesitate to delegate tasks at home and in the classroom. Encourage independence in your children and seek support from colleagues when needed.
- Utilize Prep Time: Maximize your prep periods at school to complete as much work as possible, minimizing the amount you take home.

3. Building a Support System

A strong support system is invaluable. Surround yourself with people who understand and respect your dual roles.

- Family Support: Communicate openly with your partner and family members about your needs and challenges. Share responsibilities and create a supportive home environment.

- Professional Support: Build relationships with colleagues who can offer advice, share resources, and provide emotional support. Consider forming a network of teacher-mums who can relate to your experiences.

4. Self-Care and Mental Health

Taking care of your mental and physical health is essential to effectively manage both roles.

- Set realistic expectations: Avoid striving for perfection in all areas. Set achievable goals and celebrate small successes.
- Make time for yourself: Schedule regular self-care activities, whether it's reading a book, exercising, or enjoying a hobby.
- Seek professional help: If you feel overwhelmed, consider speaking with a therapist or counsellor. Mental health is just as important as physical health.

5. Leveraging Your Skills

As a mum and a teacher, you possess a unique skill set that can be leveraged in both roles.

- Patience and Empathy: Use your patience and empathy to understand your students' needs and your children's feelings.
- Organizational Skills: Apply your classroom management skills to organise household routines and schedules.
- Creativity: Incorporate creative teaching methods into your parenting and vice versa. Engage your children in educational activities that are fun and interactive.

A small Insight into My Life

It certainly is not easy juggling the life of a mum and teacher. My boys are well-behaved, so I count myself lucky that life is not as hard as it is for others. Reuben is ten; he walks to school, enjoys playing football, gets involved in the local community, and is a true sportsman. Fabian is three and has already had a tough life: as soon as he entered the world, he continuously was in and out of hospital. I was truly exhausted—coming back after two years, leading a school and an inspection, mentally losing the plot, and doing all the jobs of a house-mum at the same time. Life took its toll and I could have done with a lot of support to get by. Being back in society was not easy; all I could hear were screams. No one knew, no one recognised, but no teacher resigns in October after waiting two years to come back. As you know, I was suffering from auditory hallucinations! What do we do when we get sick? We can't! I love cooking and having family meals, but they soon disappeared after the pandemic. Our house that was once full of joy and laughter came to an end once Dad decided he wasn't with us anymore.

Conclusion

Balancing the roles of being a mum and a teacher is a complex yet fulfilling endeavour. By embracing your dual identity, managing your time effectively, building a strong support system, prioritising self-care, and leveraging your skills, you can create a harmonious balance. Remember, it's a continuous journey of learning and adapting. Celebrate your achievements, seek support when needed, and always remember the positive impact you're making in both your family's life and your students' futures.

# CHAPTER TWENTY

# Embracing the Future

"We delight in the beauty of the butterfly but rarely admit the changes it has gone through to achieve that beauty."

—Maya Angelou

The echoes of the past are fading and are replaced by the harmonious sounds of hope and renewal. I am standing on the height of a new chapter, my spirit rejuvenated and my heart open to the possibilities that lie ahead. Burnout had once dimmed my light, but the journey through recovery has reignited a vibrant flame within me. Now as I look toward the future, I feel an unwavering sense of purpose guiding my steps. The future looks bright, and I look forward to returning to London in September 2024.

My decision to publish my book is a testament to my resilience. The manuscript, a heartfelt exploration of my struggles and triumphs, is nearly complete. Through writing, I have discovered a profound sense of release. Each word I have penned is a way to process the pain and transform it into something beautiful and inspiring. I envision this book as a beacon of hope for others, a reminder that even in the darkest times, there is always a path back to the light.

In the coming months, I will begin working in the classroom next door to Reuben's. The anticipation of being in the same school as my son fills me with joy. Reuben, with his enthusiasm, can't wait to have his mum so close by. The thought of seeing his smiling face every day is a source of immense motivation. I know that our bond will only grow stronger as we share the same space, and I look forward to being a steady presence in his daily life.

In addition to my teaching role, I am training to become a counsellor. The decision to pursue this path has come naturally to me, born from a desire to help others navigate their own challenges. My experiences have endowed me with empathy and insight, qualities I am eager to share. The counselling training is rigorous but fulfilling. Each lesson is a step closer to my goal of opening my own practice one day. I envision a safe haven where individuals can find solace and support, much like the guidance I have received during my darkest days.

Charity work has also become an integral part of my life. I am deeply involved in raising money for Oxfordshire Mind and Brain Research UK, two organizations close to my heart. These charities are dedicated to mental health and neurological research, fields I am passionate about. Through various fundraising activities, I have found a sense of community and purpose. I relish the opportunity to contribute to causes that have the potential to change lives, just as my own has been transformed.

My days are filled with purpose and positivity. I have learned to pace myself, ensuring I never again reach the brink of a burnout. Self-care is no longer an afterthought but a priority. Regular walks in nature, mindfulness practices, and spending quality time with Reuben and my Fabian are woven into the fabric of my routine. I have now cultivated a life that is balanced for my professional ambitions with personal wellbeing.

Looking forward, I feel a profound sense of gratitude. The road to recovery has been arduous, but it has led me to a place of profound self-awareness and strength. I am no longer defined by my past struggles but by the resilience and growth they have fostered. My future is a blank canvas, filled with endless possibilities and the promise of new beginnings.

With my book hopefully set to inspire others, my role in Reuben's school solidifying our bond, my counselling practice on the horizon, and my charitable efforts making a tangible difference, my future is bright. I am ready to embrace every opportunity with an open heart, guided by the wisdom I have gained. The past has shaped me, but it is the future that calls me forward, filled with hope, purpose, and the unshakable belief that I can make a difference in the world.

Even if it is a little comfort, I hope this book shows you that we are not machines. Even the most driven leaders and teachers break. I hope it teaches you all about the aftermath of suffering chronic stress and burnout. I hope it raises awareness of mental health so that the next time a dedicated colleague acts out of character, you'll go to their house and speak to them. When someone appears to be out of character, step up and talk to them. Don't let someone run out of their classroom with their belongings as if the building were on fire!

I've learned that no matter what happens, or how bad it seems today, life does go on and it will be better tomorrow!'

—Maya Angelou

I am a teacher with twenty years of experience, and this is my journey. I was a driven, ambitious leader who eventually suffered from chronic stress and burnout, which resulted in a mental episode. I suffered from dissociation, post-traumatic stress disorder, amnesia, and depression. It is also about my road to recovery, starting with talking therapy to an encounter with a medium, spiritual healing and awakening and hypnotherapy.

An author for *Nexus Education, RISE Magazine* and contributor to WomenEDs International Women's Day 2022.

Printed in Great Britain
by Amazon